what do
i do
when...

answering your **TOUGHEST**
questions about
Money

by kevin moore

Harrison House
Tulsa, Oklahoma

13 12 11 10 09   10 9 8 7 6 5 4 3 2 1

What Do I Do When?
Answering Your Toughest Questions About Money
ISBN 13: 978-1-57794-960-2
ISBN 10: 1-57794-960-9
Copyright © 2009 by Kevin Moore
P.O. Box 692032
Tulsa, Oklahoma 74169-2032

Published by Harrison House Publishers
P.O. Box 35035
Tulsa, Oklahoma 74135
www.harrisonhouse.com

Table of Contents

Introduction

What do you do when you've got questions about cash? Well, first of all, join the club. In today's world, tons of people have questions about money. An unstable economy, companies going bankrupt, and gas prices going through the roof have a lot of people scratching their heads and wondering how they can make more of the green stuff.

Well, I can't do anything about the economy or what you're going to pay at the pump, but I can give you a basic foundation about where money comes from, how you can earn it, and what you should do with it after you get it. So if money is what you're after, read on. You and your wallet will be glad you did.

May *His* best be yours,

—*Kevin Moore*

What the
Bible Says
About...

Money

Money. Money is a word we all love to say and an item we want to possess. In your pursuit of the big green, here are a few things straight from the Bible that you'll definitely want to know.

Money Comes From God

First, I want you to know that money comes from God, and He will show you how to get it. Contrary to popular belief, money doesn't grow on trees. I'm sure that's a real shocker, but it doesn't. Also, money doesn't actually come from a job, a bank, or even the federal government. In fact, money, the green stuff you want so bad, actually belongs to God.

Listen to this passage in Psalm 24:1: "The earth is the LORD'S and everything in it, the world, and all who live in it." God, the Creator of the universe, owns everything you see and even the things you don't. Money, all of it, belongs to Him. The cool thing is that God doesn't really need all that money, so He promises to give you ideas and abilities that will help you earn all the cash you need.

Deuteronomy 8:18 says, "Remember the LORD your God, for it is he who gives you the ability to produce wealth."

Did you catch that? If you remember the Lord, He will give you the ability to gain wealth, cash, coin—money.

So in your pursuit of money, remember where it comes from and ask Him to help you earn it.

You Are Not What You Have

Second, remember that you are not what you have. We love stuff, don't we? Cool clothes, nice cars, sweet houses, swimming pools, video games, and sports equipment, just to name a few. In America our closets are full of things we no longer wear, our garages are stuffed with equipment we no longer use, and our rooms are packed with games we no longer play. Why is that? Why do we have all of these things? Is it because we need them? Is it because we like them? Or is it because we think having certain things will make us better, more liked, or happier?

You see, there's nothing wrong with having stuff. In fact, there's nothing wrong with having a lot of stuff. However, it's a huge mistake when you try to define who you are as a person by the things you possess. Jesus warned us about this in Luke 12:15: "Then he said to them, 'Watch out! Be on your guard against all kinds of greed; a man's life does not consist in the abundance of his possessions.'"

Let me ask you a question: If you are what you have—what you drive, what you wear, and so forth—then who are you when you no longer have those things? Who are you when those clothes are out of style? Who are you when the car is gone? Who are you when your stuff is no longer your stuff?

You see, Jesus was letting you know that who you are as a person is much bigger than what you can ever hold in your hand. You are not—and you never will be—defined by what you have. In your pursuit of money and more stuff, remember that.

Loving Money Is a Big Mistake

Third, remember that loving money is a big mistake. Love will cause you to do some crazy things. Won't it? Through the years, I've known tons of guys who've done some pretty stupid things and gotten pretty hurt just to get the attention of a great looking girl. God's Word lets us know that loving money will cause us to do some pretty stupid things, as well. Look at 1 Timothy 6:10: "For the love of money is a root of all kinds of evil. Some people, eager for money, have wandered from the faith and pierced themselves with many griefs."

Like a guy wanting to get attention from a hot girl, people who love money will do almost anything to get it. It is not uncommon for people to lie, cheat, steal, and betray friends just to get their hands on more cash. But in the end, people who do anything to get money get a lot more pain than they bargained for.

Money Will Never Make You Happy

Fourth, remember that money can never make you happy. Money can buy you a lot of things, but money can never buy you happiness, because things can never make you happy. I remember one year I wanted an official NFL leather football for Christmas. On Christmas morning, I woke up, ran into the living room, and started ripping open one gift after another. With every gift I opened, I was hoping to see the one thing that would make me happy: an NFL football. I opened one gift, three gifts, six gifts— and no football. I opened ten gifts, fifteen gifts—and no football. Even though I had a mountain of gifts beside me, I wasn't happy, because I hadn't received my football yet.

Then it happened. My dad handed me a box. I knew it was the one. I ripped it open, and right there in my hands was an official NFL leather football. Oh, I was so happy...for about three seconds—and then I thought to myself, *This football is cool, but what I really need is a football helmet to go with it.*

Think about that for a minute. I had a pile of gifts worth hundreds of dollars right beside me. In my hand was the one thing I had always wanted. But in the end, I still wanted more.

That same thing happens to you all the time, doesn't it? You get what you've always wanted, and a few days later, you want something else. The reason is that money is great and can buy a lot of things, but things will never make you happy. Only Christ will.

Listen to these words from the apostle Paul: "I know what it is to be in need, and I know what it is to have plenty. I have learned the secret of being content in any and every situation, whether well fed or hungry, whether living in plenty or in want. I can do everything through him who gives me strength" (Phil. 4:12,13).

Paul said there were times in his life when he had everything he wanted, and other times he had hardly anything. But in both situations, rich and poor, he was happy because he had found true contentment in his relationship with Jesus Christ.

Remember: money will buy you a lot of things, but it will never buy you happiness.

Guard Your Heart Against Greed

Fifth, remember to guard your heart against greed. The Bible teaches us in Proverbs 4:23, "Above all else, guard your heart, for it is the wellspring of life." One of the big things you and I need to guard our hearts against is greed. Greed is a monster that wraps its ugly tentacles around your heart and squeezes tighter and tighter every time you see someone who has what you want. Remember: things can't make you happy; only God can do that. So the next time the tentacles of greed start to squeeze around your heart, remember these words found in Psalm 37:7. "Be still before the Lord and wait patiently for him; do not fret when men succeed in their ways."

Give and You Will Receive

Sixth, remember the principle from the Bible that when you give, you will receive. This is one of the *big* principles you need to know about money. Look at the words of Jesus in

Luke 6:38: "Give, and it will be given to you. A good measure, pressed down, shaken together and running over, will be poured into your lap. For with the measure you use, it will be measured to you."

Give. Don't be a stingy person when it comes to money. When you go out to eat with a friend, don't be afraid to buy their lunch for them. When you're going shopping, don't be afraid to pick up something for a good friend of yours. Be a giver. When you give, it always comes right back to you.

Give God What's His

Seventh, you need to remember to give God what's His. If you do, then He will give you even more. Malachi 3:8-10 says:

> Will a man rob God? Yet you rob me.
>
> But you ask, "How do we rob you?"
>
> "In tithes and offerings. You are under a curse—the whole nation of you—because you are robbing me. Bring the whole tithe into the storehouse, that there may be food in my house. Test me in this," says the LORD Almighty, "and see if I will not throw open the floodgates of heaven and pour out so

much blessing that you will not have room enough for it."

Do you like to be stolen from? I'm going to assume you don't. Well, God doesn't really care for it either. Remember the Scripture that tells us everything belongs to the Lord? Well, it's true. It does. Your birthday money, your allowance, your paycheck—it all belongs to God. However, He only asks you to give him 10 percent back. Every time you get paid, you are to give God back 10 percent of what you've earned. This is known as the tithe, which I'll explain in more depth later.

When you don't give God what belongs to Him, you are literally stealing from Him. I don't know about you, but stealing from the most powerful being in the universe doesn't sound like a good idea to me.

When you rob from God, naturally He doesn't like it. But when you give the tithe back to God, He loves it and promises to give you back even more than what you've given Him. In fact, He promises to give you more than you can even receive. When you stop and think about it, that's not too bad of a deal.

Put God First

Finally, remember to always put God first. If you do, He will take care of you. Matthew 6:33 says, "But seek first his kingdom and his righteousness, and all these things will be given to you as well."

We all want money. We all want the things it can buy for us. But the truth of the matter is that if we put our focus on the things we want, then the thing we are really after—happiness—will always be just outside our grasp.

However, when we begin to understand that everything belongs to God and we live a life worthy of the death He died for us, He (the owner of everything) will make sure that we are totally taken care of.

So in your pursuit of money, relax, do what is right, trust God, and you will be fine.

What Do I Do When...

I'm Broke?

Money. Money is something we all need but not all of us have. In fact, if you're reading this book, there's a good chance you don't have much money at your disposal and cash is not raining down on you in buckets. Well, I want to help change that. Now, I'm not saying that after reading the next five pages or so you'll magically be transformed into Donald Trump, making billion-dollar investment deals. (If that does happen, though, don't hesitate to drop a few Benjamins my way.) No, in the next few pages, you won't become a big-time investor, but you will learn some secrets about what to do when you're broke.

Broke. Now that's a word that I really don't care for. There was a time not too long ago when I was broke with a capital *B*. Man, money was tight, eating out was totally out of the question, and just taking care of the bare necessities was pretty tough. So if you are a little low on cash flow right now, I know exactly how you feel. *It stinks.*

Now, I have to say I'm not broke anymore. God is more than supplying my family's needs. We're not rich beyond our wildest imagination. You won't see my house on *MTV Cribs,* and I don't own a yacht (yet). However, we do have every-thing we need. This change from being broke to blessed didn't take place overnight, but it did happen. I want to tell you the four things I did—and you can do—to get out of the moneyless pit.

Here are four things to do when you don't have much money: ask yourself why, start working, start giving, and start saving. Let's give each of these a closer look.

Ask Yourself Why

The first thing you need to do when you don't have money is ask yourself why. Why are you broke? Is it because you're thirteen years old, don't have a job, live off your parents, and your main source of income is the gift cards you get from your grandma at birthdays and holidays? If so, that is totally understandable. You are still pretty young and what you have is, for the most part, determined by your mom and dad. However, there are still things you can do to make money. We'll talk about those later.

Why are you broke? Is it because you have a job but you spend your money as soon as you get it on the essentials of life, things like music from iTunes, movies, going out to eat, and clothes? If so, you may want to reevaluate what you consider "bare essentials."

Why are you broke? Is it because you just don't make enough money to do the things you need and want? Is it because you aren't using your money wisely?

Regardless of the reason you're broke, the first step in changing this problem is to be completely honest and ask yourself why. In fact, here's a little test you can take to figure out why you may be a little light on cash.

The Personal Broke Test

If you're honest with yourself while answering these next few questions, you just might get to the bottom line about why you're broke.

1. ### What am I doing to make money?

   What are the major sources of income in your life right now? What are you doing to make money? Are you working a job? Are you waiting on the "cash card" from Grandpa and Grandma? There's no real right or wrong answer here; just be honest with yourself.

2. ### Do I not have enough money coming in?

   Do you actually have enough money coming in to pay for the things you need and want? To answer this question, write out all your expenses: food, gas, car payment, car insurance, entertainment, etc. You might say, "Kevin, I don't have any of those types of expenses." That's okay. Think about something you want to save up for or purchase this year. After you get your list of expenses, write down how much you earn in a month or a year, then subtract your expenses from your income. Now you'll know if you have enough money coming in.

3. Do I spend the money I do have wisely?

What do you spend your money on? Do you even know? Sit down and think about what your last five purchases have been. Were they good choices? Do you regret them? A lot of times the problem is not that we don't have any money; the problem is that we make bonehead purchases.

This is a huge question. Again, be totally honest with yourself: Do you spend the money you do have wisely?

4. What would I do with a hundred bucks?

Here is a true test. If I were to come to your house and hand you a nice, new hundred-dollar bill, what would you do with it? Would you go out and spend the whole thing on that item you just have to have? Would you save some, give some, and then spend some? What would you do?

The answer to this question will shine a pretty bright light on why you may be broke. What does your answer say about the choices you make with money?

5. What kind of words am I speaking over my life?

James, one of the writers of the New Testament, once wrote that like a rudder on a large ship, our words steer the course and direction of our lives. (See James 3:3-5.) You may or may not realize it, but the words you speak have a lot to do with how much green stuff gets in and stays in your wallet.

So what kind of words have you been speaking over your life? If you've been saying words like "I'm broke," "I never have any money," "I can't afford that," or "Nothing's ever going to change," then that could be a pretty good reason why you're broke, why you don't have money, why you can't afford the things you need, and why nothing seems to be changing.

Your words have steered your money boat right into the shallow waters, and now you are getting exactly what you've been speaking: Nothing! What kind of words are you speaking over your life?

This quick little test is a great first step in understanding where you are and, more importantly, why you're in the situation you're in.

Start Working

After discovering why you're broke, the second thing you need to do is to start working. Earlier in this book, I showed you the Scripture that says, "Remember the LORD your God, for it is he who gives you the ability to produce wealth" (Deut. 8:18). God is the owner of all things, including money, and He will give you the ability to gain wealth. One of the ways God does this is through what is known as a *job*. Work.

Now, I know it would be great if all you had to do was sit by the mailbox and wait for the cash to come in. That might be what you've done in the past, but trust me when I say the twenty-five dollars from Aunt Gertrude every Christmas is not going to be enough for you to have all the things you want or need. No, if you want to stop being broke, you'll have to work.

Eight Things That Will Make You Money Right Now

No matter how old you are, here are some ideas for your first job.

1. Newspaper Route

A newspaper route may sound old school and dated, but thousands of people in your area want to read the newspaper every single morning. Why not be the one to give them what they want? It's a lot of work, but why not call a newspaper company, and start getting paid?

2. Lawn Mowing Service

Do you have a lawn mower? Do you have neighbors? If you answered yes to both of those questions, then you have a golden business opportunity literally right next door. This week, make up some flyers, begin to spread the word that you have a lawn mowing service, and start push mowing your way to mucho money.

3. Babysitting Service

Most likely you know someone who has kids. Trust me, as a married man with four kids of my own, I would love to have a trustworthy babysitter to leave my kids with so my wife, Veronica, and I could go out for a night on the town. Alone! My guess is you know someone just like me, so start letting people know you're available to serve them. Then watch the money start pouring in.

4. House-sitting Service

I've never done this, but I've known several teenagers who have. It's really a pretty good gig. You go over to a person's house while they're gone, and you live in their house for them. Cleaning it, checking the mail, making sure everything's fine. The entire time you're just living in their house, and then you get paid.

Like I said, not a bad gig.

5. Grocery Store

When I was sixteen years old, I worked at Family Fare Supermarket bagging groceries three nights a week. It was a lot of fun. I got to hang out with my friends who worked at the store, I met a lot of great people, and I got paid. Quite a few of my students from Oneighty work at a grocery store in my neighborhood, and they seem to really love it. If you have a grocery store close by, why not give it at try?

6. Camp Counselor

At Church on the Move, we have an amazing summer camp at Dry Gulch, U.S.A. Each summer, over ten thousand children and teenagers enjoy this incredible place. And each year, tons of teenagers from around the country come to Dry Gulch and serve as camp counselors.

If you have a heart for ministry and want to make a positive impact as well as a little cash, working at a summer camp may be perfect for you. Check out your local church, your denomination, and even the Internet to see if there's a camp that seems right for you.

7. Collecting Cans

I know this doesn't seem like a lot of fun, and I have to be honest: it's not. However, there are tons of cans just lying on the side of the road waiting for someone to pick them up, take them in to the recycling company, and cash them in for coins. I had a friend who made a decent amount of money each month just walking the roads around his house and collecting cans.

If you don't mind walking, you might want to try collecting cans.

Seven Things That Could Make You Money in the Future

Not everything pays you right away. In fact, if you have something you love to do and you are willing to do it for free, your talents and abilities may open the door for you to make some money in the future doing something you actually love to do. Here are seven ideas.

1. Ministry

For six years, I volunteered as the youth pastor of my church. I loved the Lord, I loved hanging out with teenagers, so working with the youth group seemed like a natural fit. Little did I know that eventually youth ministry would be the way I provided for my family.

Every day I go to the church, I can't believe I actually get paid to do what I do. If you have a heart for ministry or feel God's call on your life, maybe you should consider doing what I did and start volunteering at your church. Proving yourself faithful to the men and women God has placed in your life will open up a lot of doors for you in the future.

2. Graphic Design, Web Design, and Photography

Churches and small businesses need art pieces, photos, and Web design every single week. Start talking to people you know and showing them your work, offering to serve them for free. Take a few months, maybe even years, to hone your craft and get better at what you love. Eventually the people you're volunteering for may be able to pay you for your work. If not, you'll be improving your skills, and eventually this will open the door for other opportunities.

3. Coaching Little Kids' Sports Leagues

If you want to eventually get into coaching or a leadership role of some sort, I suggest you get plugged in with the junior sports league in your area. You'll learn how to work with parents, athletes, and other coaches. You'll make tons of connections, and by doing so, you may very well open other doors of opportunity to do what you love, and you may actually make a little money doing it.

4. Sports

Are you a good athlete? Do you excel in a certain sport? Would you excel if you really dedicated yourself to it? You know, in a few years someone your age and in your area is going to get either a partial or full-ride athletic scholarship. Why can't that person be you? Dedicating yourself and giving your best effort in the sports you play will not only get you in incredible shape, but it may even pay you in the form of a free education in the future.

5. Academic Studies

The exact same thing goes for academic studies. We had a young man at Lincoln Christian School, an incredible school that my pastor, Willie George, started several years ago, who did so well with his studies that he didn't have to pay anything for his education at a major university in Oklahoma. He didn't have to pay one dime for a college degree. His entire tuition, room and board, as well as books were 100 percent paid for by the college he chose to attend. That is the equivalent of someone handing him a check for more than eighty thousand dollars.

Whoever said studying doesn't pay didn't have a clue what they were talking about.

Start Giving

After asking yourself why you're broke and starting to work, the third thing you need to do is to start to give. Luke 6:38 says, "Give, and it will be given to you. A good measure, pressed down, shaken together and running over, will be poured into your lap. For with the measure you use, it will be measured to you." Although the context of this Scripture is actually about the way you treat the people around you, this principle of "give, and it will be given to you" also applies to money.

Basically, Jesus was saying that giving is like a boomerang. When you throw money out there—to your church, charitable organizations, people, and so forth—then what you have thrown will eventually come back to you. Now, this idea of giving away what you have goes against the grain of how people normally think, because in order to have money, we naturally think we need to keep money. However, this is a spiritual law that God, the owner of all money, has set up—and it works.

I've experienced this boomerang principle in action many times in my life. My wife, Veronica, and I have always been faithful in giving God his 10 percent back each week in the form of our tithes, and when we have the opportunity to give to an individual or a special cause, we always do. Through the years we've had so many things given to us totally out of the blue. We've had pay increases and received several checks for one thousand dollars. One time, we even had a vehicle given to us by someone we really didn't know all that well. When you give a little money to your church and you get a car in return, that is a serious boomerang!

Over the years I've seen firsthand that when you give, you always—and I do mean always—get back even more. Now I am not saying you will get a free car every time you give to God, however, if you give back to God what is His, He will always take care of you.

Now, as you're preparing to give, I want to give you three great ideas of where to throw out your money.

Three People You Need To Give To

1. God

   As mentioned earlier, all your money belongs to God, but He only asks you for 10 percent back. Whether you get a weekly paycheck, an allowance, or an occasional birthday card with money in it, make sure you always give God what is His.

2. Family

Your family is constantly giving to you, so don't be afraid to give back to them. Maybe it's a birthday present, a gift for no particular reason, or spending some time helping your little brother or sister with their homework. No matter what form it takes, practice giving back to your family. It's well worth it in the long run.

3. Others

We have a friend in Indiana who has a gift for my daughter, Mikayla, every time she sees her. Sometimes the gifts are pretty expensive, and other times they are just a little something she picked up at the store. To me, a big or small gift doesn't matter. Just the idea that this lady loves my daughter enough to think of her and give her something is priceless. We absolutely love this friend and will do anything for her and her family.

The same will be true with you and the people you give to. Everybody loves a giver, so give.

Now, don't be foolish with your money or try to buy friends. That never works. But when you have the opportunity, give someone a gift, buy them lunch, or have them over to the house and really load up on pizza and munchies. You won't regret it.

Remember: giving is a boomerang. If you're a little low on money, give. Who knows? You may just get a little back.

Start Saving

After discovering why you're broke and starting to work and give, the fourth thing you need to do is to start saving. Allow me to let you in on a little secret: If you spend all your money, you will never have any left. I know that's pretty deep, but it's true. Saving money is something most people never do. If you want to have more money, you need to be faithful and do the right thing with what little money you have right now. The right thing to do with your money is to give 10 percent to God, save 10 percent for yourself, and then live off the other 80 percent that's left.

I'll talk more about this 10-10-80 principle later, but for now the important thing to know is that you need to start saving.

Four Places You Can Save Your Money

. . . .

Here are four places you can save your money.

1. Sock Drawer

   I know this is pretty low-tech, but for someone just starting out, it's really not that bad of an idea. Get a special pouch or an envelope, and every time you get paid, put a certain amount in it, then tuck it away in your drawer. Never touch it until you are putting money in it again. You will be amazed how quickly it grows. I had a friend one time who had a buddy who had over a thousand dollars stashed away in his sock drawer. That is a lot of "stinking" money!

2. Piggy Bank

   Again, extremely low tech, but it has worked for centuries. Get a piggy bank, and put it on your dresser and start putting your money in. Don't take it out; just keep putting more in. You'll have a nice stash in no time. It will work for you if you dedicate yourself to saving your money.

3. Real Bank

A great idea is to talk to your parents and ask them to open up a savings account for you at their bank. Every time you get paid, just give your parents the money and have them deposit it in the account for you.

Many companies have automatic deposit. If you have a job, depending on where you work, this may be an option for you. How this works is that a certain amount of your check can be automatically deposited into your savings account before you even get it. I do this every week, and I've found that I never miss my savings amount because I never actually touch it.

Automatic deposit is a great way to build a nice little nest egg.

4. IRA Account

An IRA is an Individual Retirement Account that you can put money into every month or throughout the course of a year. Tons of IRA options are available to you. There are accounts for college funds, retirement funds, and even more. If you have a steady job, I suggest that you talk to your parents, find out what they are doing to save for the future, and then get something started with their accountant or money manager. This may sound complicated and over your head at first, but it's not. It's just a great way to begin to take care of what God has given you.

You may be in a situation where you are a little low on cash right now. In fact, you may be in a situation where you are flat-out broke. In either case, now you know what you need to do. Ask yourself why you are broke; then start working, start giving, and start saving. If you will do these four things, you'll begin to crawl out of the moneyless pit you've been living in.

What Do I
Do When...

I'm Looking
for a Job?

Over the next few pages, I'm going to take you through a step-by-step process to find the right job. The Bible says in Proverbs 21:5, "The plans of the diligent lead to profit as surely as haste leads to poverty."

In your search for a job, you might want to keep this Scripture in mind, because it's going to be so tempting to run out and take the very first job at the first place that's hiring and pays good money. But this is a mistake, because hasty decisions always lead to poverty.

Seven Questions To Ask When Looking for a Job

The first step in your job search is to take your time and start asking yourself some questions. Here are seven questions you can ask before you start your search.

1. ## What Do I Like To Do?

   Now, I have to warn you, work is not spelled F-U-N. Going to your job, working hard, and working smart is not always fun. So if you go into it thinking you are going to have a great time every day and your job is going to be nothing less than sunshine and rainbows, you're probably not going to last long.

That said, you are going to be spending a lot of time at the place where you work, so you might as well try to find something you enjoy doing at least a little bit.

This brings us to your first question when looking for a job: What do you like to do? Do you like being around a lot of people, or do you like to be left alone and not have a lot of interaction with several individuals? Do you like to get all sweaty and work with your hands, or are you more of the office type?

What do you like to do? When you're looking for a job, don't just look at what the pay will be. Look at what you're going to be doing, and ask yourself if you'd enjoy doing it.

2. Who's Hiring in My Area?

The second question you need to ask when looking for a job is "Who's hiring in my area?" How far are you willing to drive every day to work? Once you answer this question, start looking for jobs in this area. Is anyone close to you hiring? If so, you need to take your questions a step further.

3. What Does It Pay?

How much does the job pay? This is a huge question that you need to know the answer to up front. Before

committing to working for your boss, you need to
make sure you are willing to work for the salary you're
offered.

4. What Are the Hours?

How many hours a week are you going to be asked to
work? Will the hours be flexible? Will they work around
your schedule of sports, church, and other activities?

Again, you need to know these things up front. It's not
fair to you or your employer to take a job and then get
all upset about the hours you're working. So make
sure to answer this question before you commit.

5. What Type of Environment Is It?

Who works at the place where you're considering
working? What are they like? Will they be a positive
influence, or will they tear you down and away from
God and the things you believe? I know you need
and want money, but no job is worth losing your
faith in Christ.

6. Will It Take You Away From Activities You Love?

Again, what are the hours you'll be expected to work?
This job may pay really well, but will it take you away

from sports and other activities you love? If the answer is yes, then you need to decide which one will be more beneficial to you in the short and long run—a job or your activities.

7. Will It Take You Away From Church?

If this job will take you away from church, don't take it. Period. End of discussion. There's no reason to trade opportunities to be with friends and strengthen your faith in God just to get some money. Remember: all money belongs to God, so I don't think He would be happy with you trading Him in for the opportunity to make something He can give you. If it pulls you away from church, don't take the job.

This past summer, my family and I took a vacation to San Antonio, Texas. Man, it was really cool. We visited the Alamo, hung out with Shamu the Whale at Sea World, and hit this really huge water park. We had a blast. When we got to town, it was raining, so we decided to go to the mall and do a little shopping. But we had a big problem. We were new to the town. We had never been to San Antonio before, and there were no giant signs that read, "Follow This Road To Find the Mall." We wanted to get to the mall, but we had no clue where to even start looking. It was pretty frustrating.

That is probably how you feel right now when it comes to finding your first job. You are in the totally new place of needing to find a job, there are no giant signs up on the highway that say, "This Way to Employment," and you have absolutely no clue where to start looking.

Four Places To Look for a Job

Well, here you go. Here are four places you need to look for a job.

1. Family

   A great place to start the conversation about a job is with your family. Talk to your parents and see if there's a way that you can consistently work for them around the house or, if they have one, in their small business. If they don't have any way to help you, they may know someone who can. Again, start the conversation about a job with your family first.

2. Friends

   Do you know someone who has a business or who knows many people in the community? If so, talk to them. Let them know you're looking for a place to work and what you're interested in doing, and see if they're able to help you.

3. Church

Does your church need help in any areas of their ministry? At Church on the Move, each year we hire quite a few high school students part-time. They work backstage, with the lighting crew, and in miscellaneous jobs all throughout the ministry.

Talk to someone in your church and see if they're looking for full- or part-time help. If they are, great. If they're not, the people in the church are a great source for information and may be able to tell you who they know might be looking for help. Either way, the church is a great place to start.

4. School

You go to school every single day, right? You are already there, so why not see if they're looking for any help? Who knows? You might be able to work as a janitor, clean up after football games on the weekends, or be an assistant in the office. Don't be afraid to ask the leaders of your school to see if there is any way you can help.

5. Want Ads

If you have exhausted the options of family, friends, church, and school, now it's time to head for the newspaper. Every week, your local newspaper has a fairly large section dedicated to businesses that are hiring—the "want ads." This weekend pick up a local paper, or check if it's available online, and see who's hiring.

Before the Interview

When you find a place that seems like a good fit for you and you contact them to let them know you may be interested in working for them, they may want to bring you in for an interview. This is a way for your potential bosses to see if you will actually be a good fit for their company. However, it's also a good way for you to see if the company will be a good fit for you. Interviews can be pretty intimidating, so here are a few tips you may want to check out before you sit down for your big interview.

1. Be Yourself

The thing your potential bosses want to see just so happens to be the best thing you have going for you—and that is *the real you*. In your interview, it is very important that you not try to act like someone you think they want you to be. They just want you to be yourself, so do that.

2. Don't Brownnose

When you walk into the interview, don't spend a ton of time complimenting the boss, the company, and all the great things you've heard about them. Nobody likes a suck up, so don't be one. Walk into the room, thank them for the opportunity to meet, and then answer the questions they ask.

3. Don't Ramble

It's very important when you answer questions that you do not ramble on and on...and on and on and on.... Get the picture? Just answer the question honestly and quickly.

4. Be Honest

I heard about a college football coach one time who was hired by a really high profile university. One of the reasons he got hired was because on his résumé he wrote that he had played football at another big-time college. After he accepted the position, the university found out he had lied and fired him on the spot.

When you're looking a total stranger in the eyes and you desperately want to impress him or her, it will be very easy to start exaggerating good things and conveniently "forget" to admit bad things. This is a huge mistake, because eventually the truth will come out. So just be honest.

5. Know All That's Expected of You

Before you leave the interview, not only should you answer all of the questions but also you should ask a few of your own. You want to know what you're committing to, what their standards are, and what they are expecting from you. Knowing these things will give you a good idea whether this a true fit.

Good Luck!

Well, now that you know what to do when you're looking for a job, good luck on your search. I know God will lead you to the right place for you.

What Do I
Do When...

I Have
a Job?

You talked with family and friends. You searched the want ads. You made it through your big interview. Now you have entered the wonderful world of employment. Congratulations!

You now have a boss. You now have coworkers. You now have responsibilities. You, like millions of other people on planet Earth, now have a job. What in the world do you do now? Well, first of all you work.

Work

There are a lot of words in the English language that we love to hear. Words like "new clothes," "pizza," "college degree," and, of course, "money." All of these words flow easily off the lips—and even more easily through the fingers. But we can't have any of these amazing things unless we come into contact with a word we probably don't like to hear, much less do, and that word is *work*.

My first true job was not at McDonald's, Burger King, Wal-Mart, or even Abercrombie. No, my first real job was in the middle of a field, baling hay. My boss was a farmer by the name of Mr. Weldy. Now, Mr. Weldy was my best friend's father. He was a great guy, and he promised to pay my friend and me a pretty good chunk of money if we baled all the hay in his field and then stacked it up in his barns.

Now, this was a huge job, and it was going to take several days to get done. It was the dead of summer, and the temperature was around 100 degrees in the field. It wasn't going to be easy, but I wanted the money, so I went to work.

On the first day of baling, I arrived at the barn and found out that Mr. Weldy had hired another guy to help my friend and me bail. For the sake of this story, let's call him Larry. So John (my friend and Mr. Weldy's son), Larry, and I jumped on the tractor wagon to head out to the field.

Dude, it was hot. John and I got by the baler and started passing bales to each other and stacking them up as they came out of the shoot. Man, we were working hard. We had only been going at it for about fifteen minutes when we noticed that Larry was sitting down on the wagon, drinking some water and taking a break. It wasn't break time yet, and the bales were still coming, so John and I kept working. After a few hours in the field, one break for John and me and about five breaks for Larry, we headed back to the barn to unload all the wagons.

When we pulled the trailer into the barn, which was a cool 130 degrees, John and I started working hard at unloading all the bales. We noticed, however, that Larry wasn't any-where around. He wasn't even in the barn; he had decided to take another break. By the time "Lazy Larry" came into the barn, we had all the wagons unloaded, and the day was over.

The next day, Mr. Weldy came in the barn and asked us how the day before had gone. We told him it was hot but the day had gone pretty well, and then we showed him the work we'd done.

Mr. Weldy then informed us that it would just be John and me finishing the job—because he had fired Larry. We didn't realize it, but Mr. Weldy had been watching the whole time. He saw us working and Larry taking all of his breaks, so he decided to let good ol' "Lazy Larry" go home, where he could rest on his own time.

I'll never forget the day Mr. Weldy gave me my first paycheck. On that day, not only did I get a lot of cash; I also learned a valuable lesson. The only people who get paid are the people who work.

What do you do when you have a job? You work. Work isn't always easy, and work isn't always fun. However, work is what your boss is paying you to do. So whether you work at a restaurant, a clothing store, an office, a school, or a farm, if you want to get paid, you better get to work.

Work Hard

Not only should you work at your job, but you should work hard. One of my favorite shows on television is *Myth Busters.* If you've seen it, you know these two guys try to find out the truth about myths and urban legends that have circulated around our culture. Call me crazy, but I love watching those two science geeks try to figure out if a watermelon can really fly through an airplane windshield or if a ceiling fan will decapitate a human being. I know it's weird, but I love it.

Myths About Working Hard

Myths are all around us. There are myths about people, animals, aliens—and there are also myths about work. Here are a few myths that need to be busted about working hard.

1. Working Hard Is Doing Your Job Fast

We live in a microwave culture, don't we? You want some popcorn? Just pop it in the microwave, and you can have it in two minutes and ten seconds. You want some pizza? No problem. Slam it in the microwave, and it's yours. Oh, you're starving and need a quick snack? No worries. Just throw in some leftovers, push the button, and three minutes later, *bam,* you're scarfing down some sweet steak from last night's supper.

We have created a culture that says if it's fast, it's good. But that isn't always true when it comes to where you work. The fact that you've done your job fast doesn't always mean you've done your job right. In fact, in most cases, if you've worked very quickly, wanting to hurry up and get your job done, you probably were a little sloppy and made a few mistakes.

Whether you're bagging groceries, folding letters, or making Big Macs at McDonald's, your boss does not want you to do your job fast. They want you to do it right. So take your time. You are not a microwave.

First, master what you're supposed to do. Then as you get it down, speed up. Remember: working hard doesn't mean doing your job fast; it means doing your job right.

2. Working Hard Is Knowing What To Do

Working hard isn't knowing what to do. Working hard is doing what you know to do. So what is it that you get paid to do? Okay. Do it.

The next time you show up for work, roll up your sleeves and start doing what you know you're supposed to do. When your boss sees you doing the things he has asked you to do, he will consider you a hard worker and eventually give you a raise. If you know what to do but don't do it, you will be nothing more than a "Lazy Larry," and soon your boss will invite you to no longer work for him. In other words, *you're fired.*

3. Working Hard Is Doing What's Expected

Okay, let's say you work at a local steakhouse (man, I could go for an eight-ounce filet mignon right about now). Anyway, let's say you work as a waiter at a local steakhouse and your job is to wait on the people sitting in your area. If you serve their drinks, their appetizers, and their meal, you have done your job. You have worked and done what the people expected. However, that is not working hard. Working hard is not doing just what is expected.

Working hard is going above and beyond basic expectations and doing more than expected. If you work as a waiter, serving your guest with a smile, knowing the menu, answering all questions with confidence, getting everything to the table early, taking all empty dishes without getting in the way, and offering a heartfelt "thank you" at the end of the meal, these are ways to go above and beyond. This is working hard. So, no matter where you work, don't just work.

Work hard.

4. Work Hard Because Your Boss Is Around

It's pretty easy to work hard when you know your boss is looking, isn't it? Doing the right thing, putting things where they belong, doing what's expected of you, comes very naturally when the big fella is looking over your shoulder. That is all fine and well, but how you act and what you do on the job when the boss is not around is the true test of how good of a worker you are.

Ephesians 6:7 says, "Serve wholeheartedly, as if you were serving the Lord, not men." The bottom line is that, in the job you have right now, you do not work for your boss. You work for God. God, the Real Big Fella, is always watching. So the next time you go to work, make sure you give your best and work hard, because your Boss is always looking.

Three Reasons You Should Work Hard

Okay, let's cut to the chase here. All of this myth-busting and talking about working hard and giving your best on the job sounds really good. But let's be honest: why work hard? Why should you go to work and bust your buns every single day? I mean, what's in it for you? Well, here are three reasons why you should work hard.

1. It's What You're Paid To Do

When you buy something, you expect it to work, don't you? When you buy an iPod, a CD, or a video game system, you expect them to do what you paid money for them to do right? Well, it's the exact same way with your employer. Your boss is buying your time; she is paying you to come and do a certain thing for her. Every time you show up to work and do things halfway, you are wasting your time and your boss's money.

2. It Feels Good To Give Your Best

Through the years, I have worked for a lot of different people, and today I have a lot of people working for me. And you know what? In all the years I've been working, I have never once heard anyone say, "Boy, I gave my best at work today. Man, I wish I wouldn't have done that." Never. I've never once heard anyone complain about giving his or her best effort.

Why is that? It's because it feels good to have a task, roll up your sleeves, work hard, and get your job done. It brings a sense of purpose to your life. So this week, no matter what your job is, give your best. You will feel better for it.

3. Working Hard Eventually Pays Off Big-Time

Let's take a minute to look at the life of one of the most famous people in the Bible. Let's consider a guy named David. Now, much like you, David had a job. He had a boss. He had coworkers. He had responsibilities. David worked as a shepherd boy.

David's job was to take care of his father's sheep. Back in the day, this was a very menial position that tons of people had. Even though some would consider this a very low-level position, David took his job very seriously.

In fact, one day while David was watching his sheep, a lion came up and started to attack. David's job was to protect the sheep, so he did: he killed the lion.

Another time, a bear was on the prowl. While he was getting ready to down a few of David's sheep for dinner, David jumped in and killed it, too.

Man, this dude was watching sheep and killing animals. He wasn't afraid to give his best, now, was he?

One day, while David was taking care of his sheep, his father came up and told him he had something else he wanted him to do. Jesse, David's father, wanted him to go take some cheese to his brothers and check out how the war was going. (David's people seemed to always be fighting against these people called the Philistines; this was one of those times.) Now, delivering cheese to some guys in a war zone probably wasn't on David's shepherd boy job description, but he did it anyway. Since his job was to take care of the sheep, David went and got someone to watch his sheep while he was gone; then he grabbed some cheese, and off he went.

Once David got to the battlefield, he heard this freaka-zoid-sized man named Goliath talking smack about his God and threatening to kill all his people. So David decided that he would fight him.

Now, once again, fighting a giant was not on David's job description. He didn't have to do it, but it was something that needed to be done, so he did it.

I'm sure you know the story. David found five smooth stones, grabbed his slingshot, ran down the mountain, and killed Goliath.

Because he killed Goliath, King Saul gave him tons of cash, freed him from ever paying taxes again, and gave him his daughter in marriage. David himself eventually became king and went on to become one of the richest men in history.

Now, in terms of finding reasons why we should work hard, let's look at David's life in retrospect. If all David would have ever done was do what his job required him to do and no more, then David would have never taken the cheese to his brothers. He would have never even seen Goliath. He would have never killed Goliath. He would have never been king and rich beyond his wildest imagination. He would have spent his entire life just watching sheep.

You see, David is a great example of why you should work hard. Working hard eventually pays off big-time.

So what have you been hired to do? Do it. Give your absolute best. If you're asked to do something that isn't on your job description, don't worry about it. Just do it. Eventually it will pay off.

Work Smart

Working hard is a great thing. However, if you want to have a career and begin to make some serious coin, then you need to not only work hard; you need to work smart.

Here are a few ways you can begin to work smart.

1. Listen to Instructions

   One of the greatest skills you can ever master is the art of listening. If you will begin to listen to what your boss and the people around you tell you to do, you will make yourself a much more valuable employee.

2. Own Up to Mistakes

   As Hannah Montana once said, "Everybody makes mistakes. Everybody has those days." (Oh my gosh, I can't believe I'm actually quoting Hannah Montana.) Anyway, there are going to be times where you mess up royally. That's not good, but it is going to happen. When it does, don't make excuses, and don't push the blame off on someone else. Own up to it. Admit you messed up, and go on with your life.

3. Don't Make the Same Mistake Twice

When you make a mistake, which you will, learn from it. Remember what you did wrong, and then never do it again. Never make the same mistake twice.

4. Take Time To Do It Right the First Time

There is an old saying, "If you don't have time to do it twice, do it right the first time." Don't be in such a huge hurry. No matter what you're supposed to do, work quickly enough to be efficient, but slowly enough that you only have to do it once.

5. Think Ahead

No matter where you work, this is huge. Be the type of employee who actually uses your head. Too many people walk into work with their bodies and check their minds at the door. Don't be that type of person.

Learn to think ahead. Where are you going? What are you doing? What's coming up tomorrow, and what do you need to do today in order to be ready for it? Learn to use your mind, and you will be more valuable to the company.

6. Think Like Your Boss

Again, use your mind. What does your boss like? What does your boss expect from you? What would your boss do if he or she were in your situation? Become a student of your boss, and your boss will begin to trust you more.

Why Work Smart?

Why work smart? Why not just go into work, put in your time, collect your check, and then go home? Well, let me ask you a question. If you were a boss, and you had two employees and money for one raise, who would you give the raise to? The person who shows up and does nothing more than is expected, or the person who listens to instructions, owns up to mistakes, never makes the same mistake twice, does things right the first time, thinks ahead, and thinks just like you? That's what I thought—and that's why you need to work smart.

What Do I
Do When...

I Get
My First
Check?

There's nothing like getting your very first paycheck. You've worked hard all week. You've done what you were supposed to do, and now you're getting paid for it. It's incredible! But now that you have all this money in your hands, what are you going to do with it? What should you do with it?

Well, to answer that question, let me ask you a question. Have you ever seen a house being built, like on *Extreme Makeover: Home Edition*? It's pretty cool to watch as the foundation is poured, the frame is constructed, the roof is put on, the electrical and drywall work is done, and the house is completed. I love building things and watching things be built. I guess that's why I worked as a draftsman drawing houses for several years.

Well, one time there was a home being built pretty close to mine, and I passed it almost every day. As I drove by, I would watch as the construction on the home slowly progressed. After the foundation was poured, the workers began to put up the frame. It was a huge two-story house. The roof line was really cool. The windows were monstrous. I could tell this place was going to be sweet.

One night we had a pretty decent storm—nothing major, but a little bit of rain and wind. I didn't think much about it and went to bed. The next day, I woke up, got ready for work, and headed out the door.

As I drove to work that day, I looked out my car window to see how the house was coming. I looked to my left to take a look, and it was gone.

When I say *gone,* I mean *gone.* It wasn't there. The entire house had blown over, and the only thing left was a pile of busted lumber. It looked like pictures I've seen when a tornado hits a trailer park. It was a mess.

Before the storm, the house looked incredible. However, though you couldn't tell from a distance, the frame wasn't put together right. When the storm hit, the whole thing just blew over.

Like the house that I watched being built that then crumbled to the ground, a lot of people look like they have it all together. We see them from a distance and think their lives must be pretty sweet. They have cars, clothes, and concert tickets. But when the car breaks down, the bills start piling up, or they lose their job, everything they have comes crashing to the ground like this two-story house that wasn't built very well.

Here's the point. You want to make something pretty sweet out of your life, and it's going to take money to do it. Once you have money, you need to start building a financial framework that will weather any storm.

You see, it would be great if life were always sunny and perfect, but it's not. The truth of the matter is that small storms will hit your wallet sometimes, and if you haven't done things right up till that point, you and your pocketbook will be feeling some serious pain.

So how do you build a strong financial framework? Well, it can all be summed up in three numbers: 10, 10, 80. If you will use these numbers correctly, you will have a great start. Here's how you build your financial foundation with 10, 10, 80.

Give 10 Percent Back to God
●●

Earlier in the book, I wrote about giving 10 percent of what you make back to God. This is called the tithe, and it's the first thing you should do with your paycheck. I won't spend a lot of time explaining what the tithe is, because I've already done that. However, here are a few reasons why you should tithe.

1. It Belongs to God

Remember: "The earth is the LORD's, and everything in it" (Ps. 24:1). So if you stop and think about it, your check—all of it—actually belongs to Him. God is just asking that you give Him back 10 percent of what He has given you.

When you give a portion of the money God gave to you back to Him, you are showing God that you love and trust Him. When He sees that He can trust you with money, He will give you back even more.

2. You'll Have More Money

One thing you need to understand is that when you get paid and cash your check, you are holding more than money; you are actually holding seeds.

You see, money is a seed that, if planted, will actually produce a harvest of more seeds. So when you give the tithe back to God, you are planting a seed in the ground that will give you more seeds (money) back.

On the other hand, when you spend all your money, it's like you're eating all your seeds and there is nothing more to plant. Because you don't plant anything, you don't harvest anything—and all your money is gone.

So if you want to have more money, which I'm pretty sure you do, plant some seeds by tithing.

3. It's the Right Thing To Do

As a Christ follower, you have a responsibility to do the right thing. Period. All throughout Scripture, God instructs you to bring Him the tithe. If you do not do it, you are disobeying God. So when you get your first check, do the right thing by giving God what rightfully belongs to Him.

Now, you might be reading this and thinking, *All of this sounds great and makes total sense, but how do I tithe? Where do I take it?*

Well, when you get your check, take the gross amount (this is the amount before taxes are taken out), and figure out what 10 percent would be. Once you have the amount, set it aside. Once you have set it aside, bring it to your local church, and put it in the offering bucket.

You might think, *Okay, I guess I can do that, but what does the church do with God's money? Do they put it all in a huge box and UPS it up to heaven so God can have it?*

Well, no that is not how it works. You see, God uses the local church as an organization to show people how good, gracious, and kind He really is. So the tithe you give goes to the church; the church then uses that money and continues to make an impact for Christ in your community.

Without the tithe, the church would not be able to afford a building, lighting, equipment, and pastors. When you give your tithe, you are helping God's church be able to do what He designed it to do: make the world and the people in it a better place. So when you get your check, tithe.

Save 10 Percent for Yourself

After giving your first 10 percent to God, the second thing you should do with your paycheck is save 10 percent for yourself. In Deuteronomy 28, we find that if we obey God's commands, everything we do will be blessed. It says that God will bless our bread basket and our bread bowl (v. 5). Now, that is a pretty weird phrase for today's culture, isn't it? I mean, what in the world is a bread bowl? I know

Panera Bread makes a great broccoli cheddar soup bread bowl, but I don't think that's what God was talking about.

For years, I didn't understand this phrase. In fact, back in the day, I used to wonder if "blessing your bread basket and bread bowl" meant God would bless the two pieces of bread I had in the cupboard on Monday and turn it into three pieces on Tuesday.

But in reality, God was not talking about Panera Bread or about magically multiplying bread at all. You see, way back in Bible times, people had bread they'd use every day. They would save unbaked bread with yeast in it to bake more bread another day.

Now, you may not realize it, but you and I do the same thing, just not with the bread we eat. We do this with the bread we spend: money. So what God was talking about in Deuteronomy 28 was that if we obey Him, He will bless our checkbook (the money we need today) and our savings account (the money we are saving up for big purchases or emergencies).

One important thing you need to remember is that God cannot bless something that does not exist. So if you don't save any money, you are not giving God any "bread" to bless. But if you give God even a little, He can easily turn it into a lot.

Think about the story in the Bible where Jesus fed five thousand people with some fish and bread. How did He do it? Did He place a huge order at Long John Silver's, have it all delivered, then feed all the people with it? No. What did He do? He took five loaves and two fish that a little boy gave him, blessed it, multiplied it, and fed the people with it. In fact, the Bible says that the little boy had twelve baskets full of leftovers to take home to his family.

Now, let's figure this out and see how the boy turned out in this transaction. This kid gave Jesus five loaves and two fish. This kid ate his meal and then walked away with twelve baskets of food. He gave God a little and God turned it into a lot. I don't know about you, but that sounds like a pretty good deal.

The same is true with your money. If you live a life that is sold out to Christ and you start putting even a little bit of money into a sock drawer, piggy bank, or savings account, God will turn your little into a lot.

So when you get your first check, give God something to work with and save at least 10 percent. You will be amazed how fast it grows.

Live Off the Rest

After giving 10 percent to God, saving 10 percent, the third thing we need to do is live off the remaining 80 percent of our paycheck. Let's say you got paid and you're holding a check for two hundred dollars. You go to church on Sunday and give God His tithe (twenty dollars). You take out twenty dollars and put it in your savings account. That leaves you with one hundred sixty dollars. Right?

Well, what do you do with this money? I don't know. You tell me. It's your money, so do whatever you want with it! You've worked hard all week, you've earned your money, and so you get to have fun deciding what to do with it.

Now, don't be stupid and go out and blow the whole thing on squirt guns, pop tarts, and some sweet striped socks. No, you need to think through what you need, what you want to do, and what you want to buy.

Remember: 10 – 10 - 80

You want to build something great out of your life. So start now. Take your very next check and begin building a strong financial frame, one that will get you through tough times. It's all found in these three numbers: 10, 10, 80. Give God 10 percent, save 10 percent, and then live off the 80 percent that's left. Do this, and your life won't just look good from a distance; it will be good from up close.

What Do I
Do When...

I Want
a Raise?

Do you remember when you were a little kid? Back in the days of action figures and Barbie dolls, all you had to do was ask for something and you would get it. When you were a toddler sitting in your high chair stuffing peas up your nose, if you pointed at something on the table and jabbered a few words, your parents would hand it to you. Way back in the day when you were in love with a giant purple dinosaur named Barney, all you had to say was you wanted a Happy Meal and your parents would pull into good ol' McDonald's and grab you one. If you needed new cleats for football, some pom-poms for cheerleading, or a new outfit for school, your parents, grandparents, or friends of the family were always there to give you exactly what you needed.

Because of the way we were treated when we were children, a lot of people are under the impression that life will always be this way. Someone will always be there to serve their every need and give them exactly what they want, when they want it. If you are one of these people, I'm sorry to burst your bubble, but you are sadly mistaken.

You see, one of the greatest lessons you can ever learn is that in the real world, no one gives you anything. If there is something you want, you are going to have to earn it.

So with that being said, what do you do when you want a raise?

You earn it.

When it comes to money, you need to understand that if you *want* more, you are going to have to *do* more. A lot of people don't like that. In fact, tons of people have the mentality that if they want more, someone should just give it to them. But again, in the real world, the world of thirteen years old and up, no one gives you anything. If you want more, you are going to have to earn it.

How? How do you earn more? Well, you do more. In fact, if you really want more, you have to do a lot more.

More Effort

If you want a raise, the first thing you need to do is make more of an effort at work. One time, I walked into a store at the mall. I saw customers everywhere but no employees. In fact, there was not one worker in the room at all. I kept looking around wondering where the workers were, when I noticed something moving behind the cash register. I peeked my head over the counter and saw the store clerk sitting Indian style on the floor, talking on her cell phone. She looked up at me like I was a weirdo and really interrupting her, so I turned and walked out of the store.

Let me ask you a question: Does this girl deserve a raise? Well, unless her boss was paying her to sit behind the counter and talk on the phone, I don't think a raise was coming her way anytime in the near (or distant) future.

Remember, in the real world, people don't give you anything. You have to earn it. If you want a raise, answer this question: What are you doing to earn one? When was the last time you went to your job and gave your absolute best effort? Honestly, when was it?

When you begin to give more effort, your boss will notice and give you more money.

More Production

If you want a raise, the second thing you need to do is produce more. Wherever you work, you're being paid to produce something your boss can sell for money. If you work at a clothing store, you're being paid to assist people in buying more clothes. If you work at a fast-food restaurant, you're being paid to produce food very quickly for customers. If you work at a farm, you're being paid to help produce, well *produce.* You know—fruits, vegetables, and grains.

The more you produce, the more money the company you work for makes. The more money the company makes, the greater chance you have of getting more money, *aka* a raise.

So if you want a raise, don't just do the bare minimum. Work harder and smarter in order to produce more. More sales, more shirts, or more sandwiches. When you do, a raise just might be around the corner.

More Time

If you want a raise, the third thing you can do is spend more of your time at work. Remember: you're being paid to produce something. Every once in a while, your company will need you to work more than what you originally agreed to, in order to complete a job.

Maybe you normally work fifteen hours a week after school, but your boss comes up to you and says he needs you to work an extra two hours on Saturday. How do you react to this? Do you sulk and pout? Do you get all upset?

Or do you do your best to keep a great attitude and do what you've been asked to do?

When it comes time to decide who gets a raise, your boss is going to think of the people who value the company and aren't afraid to do what's necessary to get the job done.

If that's you, you could be getting a raise. So don't be afraid to put in some more time, because soon you could be getting some more cash.

More Value

If you want a raise, the fourth thing you can do is to make yourself more valuable to your employer. *Pimp My Ride* on MTV was one crazy show. These guys would take old beater cars that were absolute junk worth only a few hundred dollars, and they'd turn them into sweet street machines worth thousands.

What happened to make the cars worth so much money? Well, some very valuable things were added to them. Things like new carpet, new seats, new stereo systems, video games, and crazy stuff like fish bowls. All of these items added value to the vehicles and made them worth more money.

How about you? Do you add value to the place you work? When you are there, do more things get done? Do more sales get made? Do things run more smoothly?

Do you add value? When you do, your boss will add to the amount you get paid.

More Knowledge

If you want a raise, the fifth thing you can do is to gain more knowledge about your work.

Who makes more money: a trash man or a brain surgeon? If you say trash man, you may need to go see a brain surgeon. Now, let me just add this, there is absolutely nothing wrong with being a trash man. In fact, I've heard of some very wealthy people who run trash collecting businesses. However, without any doubt, a brain surgeon makes a whole lot more money than a trash man.

Why? Well, brain surgeons are extremely knowledgeable. They're specialists, and specialists always get paid more than the average worker.

So when it comes to your job, are you an average worker or are you a specialist? If you will become more knowledgeable about what you do, you will begin to move up the pay scale.

More Commitment

If you want a raise, the sixth thing you can do is to make a longer commitment to your work. One of the biggest reasons people don't get a raise is that they don't stay in one place long enough to get one. A lot of people take a job without any real commitment to the place where they're working.

I've heard tons of teenagers through the years say things like this: "Oh, I'll work here for the summer, and then I'm done," or "Well, I'll stay here until the place I really want to work hires me," or "I guess I'll keep working here until something bigger or better comes along."

Because they're not committed, they don't give their best. And because they don't give their best, they don't add value to the workplace. And because they don't add value, they don't get a raise.

If you want to get more from your boss, you have to show that you're committed to what you're doing.

Fishing With More
Than One Pole

Here is the seventh thing you can do to help you on your path to a larger payday: Fish with more than one pole in the pond.

I absolutely love fishing. In fact, a few days ago my son and I went fishing with a friend and caught some mongo catfish monsters. It was a blast.

I remember one time quite a few years ago, I took my son Jordan fishing at a family friend's house. This guy had his own private pond. It was pretty big. In fact, it was border-line a lake. It was huge. He had it totally stocked with all kinds of fish, so I had a pretty good idea that we would catch at least a little something.

Well, we started fishing. Man, we had a great time sitting on the bank, each of us with one pole in the water. After a little while, our friend came up with another pole in his hand and said, "Hey, Kevin, there are tons of fish in my pond. Why not put another pole in the water and double your chances at catching a good one? So I did, and sure enough a few minutes later I hooked into a huge large-mouth bass. To this day, I've never caught a larger fish.

At the risk of seeming like a broken record, I want to remind you yet again that "the earth is the Lord's and everything in it" (1 Cor. 10:26). "It is he who gives you the ability to produce wealth" (Deut. 8:18). You see, it's almost like the earth is God's giant fishing pond and He has it totally stocked with money—money that all belongs to Him—and God in His goodness has invited you to sit down at his pond and fish for cash.

Now, most people are like me at my friend's house. They fish with only one pole in the water. By this I mean they have only one job, and they expect this one job to give them all the money they'll ever need.

But you see, like me sitting on the side of the bank, you'll increase your chances of getting more money if you fish with more than one pole in the water. What I mean by that is you will make more money if you have two sources of income—two jobs.

Now, I am not suggesting that you get two jobs at the expense of your academics. But let's say you've got the summer off school and you've got a ten-hour-per-week job mowing lawns. And let's assume you want more money. Well, have you thought of taking on another job?

You might read this and think, *Two jobs? Man, that is a lot of work! I don't want to work that hard! I just want to get more money.*

Well, if that is your attitude, you need to read this passage found in Proverbs 10:4: "Lazy hands make a man poor, but diligent hands bring wealth." Scripture teaches that if you want wealth—more money—you have to work hard.

Again, nobody is going to give you anything. You are going to have to earn it. I have learned that if you really want to make more money, you can work at more than one single job. In fact, right now as I sit at God's money pond, I have four fishing poles in the water.

Church. I have the honor of being the youth pastor at Church on the Move in Tulsa, Oklahoma, where I serve the vision of my pastor, mentor, and friend, Pastor Willie George. Reaching out to teenagers in the Tulsa area with the good news of Jesus Christ is my main agenda in life and also my main source of income for my family.

Speaking. About four to five times per year, I travel and speak at youth and leadership conferences around the country. Again, this is something I love to do, and it does not in any way seem like a job. However, I do get paid to travel and speak.

Writing. I spend at least one night per week, as well as most Saturday mornings, writing. The Lord has opened the door for me through my good friends at Harrison House to write books for teenagers and youth leaders around the country.

Consulting. Each month I work with youth pastors from around the country to help them develop their students and ministry into all God's called them to be.

Now, each and every one of these is something I absolutely love doing. However, by no means is it easy to juggle these four jobs along with the rest of my life. I do it, first, because I love it and know this is what God has called me to do. And I do it because each of these things is a pole in the water of God's pond, and every week God blesses me with more because I'm willing to diligently work for Him.

The exact same can happen with you. Have you ever thought of working more than one job? Well, maybe you should. If you have a job working at a store, restaurant, school, or farm, that is your first priority because it's your main source of income. However, you could also talk to your parents about working for them around the house, for even a small amount of spending cash.

One of the best things to do for extra income is to take something you love to do and do it so well that people will pay you for your services. I had a student in one of my youth ministries who made amazing jewelry. She was constantly making necklaces, bracelets, and anklets for herself. Her friends started wanting some, so she started a small business in her living room making jewelry. The word started to spread, and she made a lot of extra money doing something she loved to do.

In fact, today I know teens who detail cars, make videos, and do graphic design as a second source of income—a second fishing pole, if you will. You can do the same. In fact, if you really want more money, you should. Just work hard, and you'll have the cash you need.

Conclusion

We all want cash, and I hope this book has given you some good tips for making it and using it well. You've learned what to do when you're broke, when you're looking for a job, when you have a job, when you get your first check, and when you want a raise. If you'll follow these principles, you're going to be doing great for cash.

Depending on how old you are, you may be reading this, thinking, *I can't do anything with any of this stuff right now. I mean, I can't even drive a car yet.* That's okay. You're ahead of the game. Save this book, put these principles in your heart, and when the time is right, put them to work for you.

Whether you've never had a job, or you've been working for years, remember: If you want something, you have to earn it. If you want more money, start doing more on the job you currently have and don't be afraid to put more fishing poles in God's pond.

Prayer of Salvation

God loves you—no matter who you are, no matter what your past. God loves you so much that He gave His one and only begotten Son for you. The Bible tells us that "...whoever believes in him shall not perish but have eternal life" (John 3:16). Jesus laid down His life and rose again so that we could spend eternity with Him in heaven and experience His absolute best on earth. If you would like to receive Jesus into your life, say the following prayer out loud and mean it from your heart.

Heavenly Father, I come to You admitting that I am a sinner. Right now, I choose to turn away from sin, and I ask You to cleanse me of all unrighteousness. I believe that Your Son, Jesus, died on the cross to take away my sins. I also believe that He rose again from the dead so that I might be forgiven of my sins and made righteous through faith in Him. I call upon the name of Jesus Christ to be the Savior and Lord of my life. Jesus, I choose to follow You and ask that You fill me with the power of the Holy Spirit. I declare that right now I am a child of God. I am free from sin and full of the righteousness of God. I am saved in Jesus' name. Amen.

If you prayed this prayer to receive Jesus Christ as your Savior for the first time, please contact us on the web at **www.harrisonhouse.com** to receive a free book.

Or you may write to us at

Harrison House

P.O. Box 35035

Tulsa, Oklahoma 74153

About Kevin Moore

Kevin Moore is the youth pastor of Oneighty®, the youth ministry of Church on the Move in Tulsa, Oklahoma. With more than 16 years experience in youth ministry, Kevin's passion in life is to introduce teenagers to the person of Jesus Christ and help them walk out their faith in a real and personal way.

Throughout the year, Kevin travels and speaks at leadership and student conferences around nation. The biblical principles he shares are proven to work in any size church or city.

Kevin and his wife Veronica have been married for 17 years. They have four children: Jordan 16, Logan 13, Mikayla 9, and Lilly Grace, 1 year old.

You can contact Kevin Moore at
growmoore@gmail.com
www.twitter.com/kevinmoore180
www.facebook.com/kevinmoore180
P.O. Box 692032
Tulsa, OK 74169-2032

Read Kevin's blog at www.kevinmoore.tumblr.com

Please include your prayer requests
and comments when you write.

Other Books in the What Do I Do When? Series

What Do I Do When—Answering Your Toughest Questions About God

Kevin Moore encourages you to seek God for yourself in the Scriptures and in your own heart, plus answers questions like: "Why do bad things happen to good people?" and "What do I do when I'm a Christian but the feelings are gone?" You will discover amazing things about God and learn a lot about yourself along the way.

What Do I Do When?

Answering Your Toughest Questions About God

978-1-57794-959-6

What Do I Do When—Answering Your
Toughest Questions About Friends

Filled with humor and grounded in God's Word, Moore
answers your tough questions about friends including:
"What do I do when my friends don't want Jesus?" and
"What do I do when my friend is mean?" You will be
empowered to act in love and common sense with

Moore's comical, yet strong, biblical advice.

What Do I Do When?

Answering Your Toughest
Questions About Friends

978-1-57794-962-6

What Do I Do When—Answering Your Toughest Questions About Sex, Love, and Dating

From questions like "What do I do when my parents won't let me date?" to "What do I do when my date wants to get physical?" you will find the answers backed by God's Word and in the context that addresses today's issues.

What Do I Do When?

Answering Your Toughest Questions About Sex, Love, and Dating

978-1-57794-961-9

Fast. Easy.
Convenient.

For the latest Harrison House product information and author news, look no further than your computer. All the details on our powerful, life-changing products are just a click away. New releases, E-mail subscriptions, testimonies, monthly specials—find it all in one place. Visit harrisonhouse.com today!

harrisonhouse

The Harrison House Vision

Proclaiming the truth and the power

Of the Gospel of Jesus Christ

With excellence;

Challenging Christians to

Live victoriously,

Grow spiritually,

Know God intimately.